Poetry
In
Life

Daisy Mae Easton

ISBN-10:1505659035

ISBN-13: 978-1505659030

Second Edition

DEDICATION

I dedicate this book to my son, Christopher William Frank, for the inspiration and love that he has given me. He has always been a joy to be around and has given me a life that is full of pride for having been his mother. For as his mother I see the world not only through my eyes, but through his as well.

CONTENTS

ACKNOWLEDGMENTS

I want to thank all the teachers, co-workers, students, friends, and family, who have been an inspiration for my writing, and a blessing in my life.

TEACHERS

Educators come in every shape,
Size, age, height, and nationality,
Background, education, and hometown,
Vocation and personality.

Some inspire, coach, and some may preach,
Even drill, and model behavior,
Show patience, test, correct, grade, and teach,
Act sad, happy and not show favor.

Every teacher has a goal to reach
Teaching our children to be their best,
Showing how to use God given skills
Guiding them through a standardized test.

For them to run the nation and world
Our future demands they be ready,
With common sense and family values
To keep the economy steady.

We are training our new replacements
So when educators do retire,
Leaders for the next generation
Can guide the students to aspire.

PAYDAY

Our days are spent just working.
We wait to get paid and when
Figuring out our budget
Our money is gone again.

The pay is much too little
And earmarked before it comes.
We calculate the outflow
Adding up the total sums.

And, if only once a month
We estimate our bills due,
Then go out for groceries
The overdrafts can ensue.

Where does it all go? Who knows?
How are the funds depleted?
We know the banks get big fees,
Bank's purposes defeated.

Where did it all go so fast?
And, why are we always short?
When did the cost of living
Become such a payday sport?

THE EARLY TEXAS SKY

The trees are standing still today
And the weather is oh, so fine.
Red ribbons in the sky at play
Bright blues and rosy pinks align.

Some miracle at daybreak's clock,
A pink circle against the cloud
Surrounds me on my morning walk,
Finds me wishing there were a crowd.

The skies a red and blue display
Beautiful and splendid to see.
Rising sun burns colors to gray
Fading the pink clouds around me.

I alone saw the early hues
Of the beautiful sky that day.
Encircling pink, reds and blues
That so quickly faded away.

THE CHILD WITH SPECIAL NEEDS

The child is dear who cannot speak.
But maybe he can spell
Or learn to use a computer
And do so very well.

Another child you see fidget,
Wiggle or can't sit still
Who may need some special training,
And still exerts strong will.

And then you see the child who's blind
Who knows your voice and walk
Can't hold a conversation but
Repeats you when you talk.

The child who's not able to hear
Says the alphabet wrong
Then looks for hugs and holds your hand
And sings his own sweet song.

The precious children I speak of
Have disabilities.
But, the one who writes C's backwards
Builds computers with ease.

The child who may seem so anxious
He sometimes shouts and screams,
Can remember names and numbers
With accuracy it seems.

The child who is not a reader
Is best at math today,
With books on tape or Internet
Finds knowledge a new way.

Another child with special needs
Loves art and draws for you.
Don't ask him for his drawing pad
Or you may make him blue.

A child who cries or talks too much,
The kids who gets too loud,
Someday famous in their own right
And won't we all be proud.

Because children all have talent
And yet they won't go far,
Without love and understanding,
Accepting who they are.

With extra training they can be
All they are meant to be,
Amid Special Educators
And, help from you and me.

SOMEONE SPECIAL

A young boy waits in the new morning dawn
For the school bus to come rolling along.
He wears a ball cap and carries a ball.
He's cute and sassy and not very tall.

His lip quivers in the cool morning air.
Winter is coming but he doesn't care.
He loves all sports and his favorite teams
Are Cowboys, Mavericks and Rangers it seems.

He has lots of friends that call him by name
Can't wait to see him and star in his game.
The coaches all like to see him play ball
This kind freckled child who's not very tall.

Some days he's absent, but with good reason.
No regular doctor trip this season.
He sees the doctor, then goes back to school
With a new wheelchair, the color is cool.

It's royal blue and it really goes fast.
He's very proud that he got it at last.
Out on the playground you'll see him this year
In his sporty wheelchair feeling no fear.

He can make two points. He throws the football.
He's great at Rat-Race. He loves Roller-ball.
He's quick retrieving the ball on the ground.
Get out of his way; he's on that rebound!

TIME CHANGE

It's the early alarm
I am out of the bed.
The hot morning shower's
Running over my head.

Next, I towel dry my hair
Then use the hair dryer.
I am rushing around
Like the house caught fire.

Quickly put on my clothes
And I rush out the door.
Can't wait for Saturday
To come around once more.

My long hair is still damp.
This bus ride is bumpy.
The old lady driver
Is loud and she's grumpy.

My hair is really straight
I wish it were curly.
Now we pass the bank clock,
It's an hour early?

My, the clocks have all changed
As a matter of fact.
I suppose I forgot
To re-set my clock back.

I have time for breakfast
That's not such a bad deal.
Wow! If I could find eggs,
Truly, that would be real.

WEE HOURS

Red lights flashing as the road ahead curves.
Raindrops are falling as the sign detours.
Headlights glaring in the early morn mist.
The dark horizon seeming moonlight kissed.

Driver fights to see oncoming traffic.
Reflections of light make objects manic.
Caution, caution flashes the yellow light.
Orange striped barrels line the construction site.

The bird's silhouette passes overhead
Flying up in the sky with wings outspread.
A fresh damp sea smell in the morning breeze.
Dripping leaves twinkle on the new dawn's trees.

Bright lights reflect like mirror on the lake.
Raindrops sprinkle making the puddle's wake.
Autumn coolness paints the dark trees passé.
'Open' flashes at the Donut Café.

A NOVEMBER SCHOOL DAY

It was a bleak November day.
The trees were bending in the wind.
Children could not go out to play.
The playground was empty again.

It had been a rainy morning,
Grey skies and sporadic showers.
Autumn colors were a warning.
Cold and stormy early hours.

The children had indoor recess
With snacks everyone brought from home.
The teachers all prayed for sunshine
Or a really gigantic storm.

The morning passed uneventful
The afternoon kind of a blur.
All got another day older
And maybe a bit more mature.

FIFTH GRADE MATH CLASS

"The sum-of-the-digits are divisible
And, divisibility rules apply great.
Finish your divisibility paper
Then please turn it in, you don't want to be late."

The assigned paper is for a grade in math.
And the astute math students will all agree,
Even numbers are divisible by two
Add the sum of digits to divide by three.

So everyone quietly starts their paper.
Classical music plays softly in the back..
And the teacher once more gets busy grading
Their tests and papers from a really big stack.

The teacher looks up, frowns and snaps her fingers
As she sees students are talking and wriggling.
She tells them once more they need to be quiet.
"Please don't talk, stay seated and stop that giggling!"

"Some of you are not simplifying," she said.
They quiet down nicely to re-calculate.
The teacher finishes her grading quickly
And then gives the new lesson after the break.

BASEBALL

In baseball you hit the ball with a stick.
If you miss three times you are out, and then
You have to sit on the bench for a while
And wait until it is your turn again.

Then, you can get back in the game once more.
They call you to bat and you hit the ball.
You have to run round the bases to score.
They'll tag you to get you out so don't stall.

If they do not tag you, you are not out.
When you score more points than the other team
You get a huge, baseball trophy, this big!
Metals, a pizza party and ice cream!

Catchers should wear a mask, mitt and chest pad,
Outfielders a glove, cap and jersey too.
The best part of all is to hit the ball
And players must wear cleats instead of shoes.

THAT'S WHAT YOU GET

"Coach, I threw-up going on the merry-go-round too fast!"
"That's what you get," said the coach.
"That kid I was tripping, fell right on me as he went past!"
"That's what you get," said the coach.

"On the playground, I tackled my friend and I bit my tongue!"
"That's what you get," said the coach.
"In grabbing the big ball from my teammate, I bent my thumb!"
"That's what you get," said the coach.

"I was hanging upside down on the monkey bars, and fell!"
"That's what you get," said the coach.
"I was sliding down on the bleachers, and I hit the rail!"
"That's what you get," said the coach.

"I was pulling hard on Freddie's coat, and fell on my back!"
"That's what you get," said the coach.
"I was too close to the batter and got hit by the bat!"
"That's what you get," said the coach.

"I was swinging and jumped off the swing, and tore up my knee!"
"That's what you get," said the coach.
"I climbed up the slide and a student coming down kicked me!"
"That's what you get," said the coach.

"I threw fake punches at my best friend, and I hit the wall!"
"That's what you get," said the coach.
"I sat on the floor, got hit in the face in roller-ball!"
"That's what you get," said the coach.

"I think I ate too much at lunch, and my belly hurts bad!"
"That's what you get," said the coach.
"I was running down the hallway and I fell!" said the lad.
"That's what you get," said the coach.

TWEET! TWEET! TWEET! GOES THE COACHES
WHISTLE AT P. E.

COMPLIANT OR NON-COMPLIANT

"Do the lesson as the directions say,"
Said the teacher to the student.
"What if I want to do things my own way!"
Said the non-compliant student.

The teacher's observing the student's work
Even though the child's steps are wrong
Finds that the student's answers are correct
So the student's knowledge is strong.

The non-compliant student does more work
Doing the work just as he likes
Then, quickly changes the assignment's end
To avoid the teacher's requites.

Seeing the student is non-compliant
Does he deserve less than an A?
Maybe the student is just creative,
Could be he knows a better way.

Must we be flexible to see the views
Or not be too hasty to mark
A lower grade on those who don't comply
With methods, discounting a lark?

Or, possibly a five-point penance mark
For his being non-compliant?
To make him accountable for his steps
Chastised for being defiant.

ONLINE ROMANCE

We met by mere chance on the Internet one day.
And, we chatted and e-mailed the evening away.
He will say things to me to make my day better.
No need to send ink on a card or a letter.

This wonderful man is bright and he is youthful.
And he tells me things that I know to be truthful.
He tells me I'm beautiful and calls me sweetheart.
It really makes my day when he sends an e-card.

He's cheerful and loving and always seems happy
To hear me on the phone, and now it sounds sappy
But the best part of all is we talk and share thoughts.
We've become such good friends, and we have late night talks.

We are both middle-aged and been married before.
Both know of heartache and disappointment galore.
Our children are all grown and have their own careers.
And the gray in our hair has been earned through the years.

The site where we met was a senior dating site.
We saw a few others not impressive or right.
In reading his profile, I saw he was a catch.
After phoning and chatting we realized a match.

He's been so polite and we talk almost daily.
I think of him often, always positively.
It has been a few months of not seeing his face.
Now our hope is to meet soon and maybe embrace.

Then, if all works out well and we want to know more.
We will spend time together, our bond to explore.
The sky is the limit as we face our old age.
And, will we find a true love on this our last stage?

CAPTAIN OF THE FOOTBALL TEAM

He was an honorary Captain.
The high-school cheerleaders knew his name.
His face appeared in the newspaper.
He showed up for every football game.

He ran in front on the football field
Of the players all dressed in their gear.
To guarantee the luck of the game
And to rally the team's fans to cheer.

This happy team player made the rounds.
He was always friendly and cheerful.
You'd never guess he was born with Downs
Always smiling and never tearful.

He had so many good friends at school.
We wonder how he is as a grad.
Remembering how he was so cool
And thinking what a good time he had.

He worked part-time at Wendy's Café
After school, during his high-school days.
And, everyone remembers him there
For his great big smile and funny ways.

He graduated last year and still
You'll see him at every football game.
High school's over for this football star
But, he attends all games just the same.

TEACH IT FORWARD

We can work, eat, love, sleep, play and pray.
Enjoy good music, company, a summer day.
Tell someone we love them everyday,
Remind them they are beautiful in every way.

Work's a great escape from family grief.
Too much work can often steal our time, such a thief.
Our loved ones soon will all become grown.
Short are the years we have with them, then we're alone.

Enjoy food from different cultures, taste
Every new sensation and flavor, without waste.
People do go hungry, some are poor.
Donate food and time to the community store.

Read books, learn something new everyday.
Find new hobbies to entertain the rainy day.
Help someone who needs help, be a friend.
Visit someone, a good fellowship to attend.

Sleep is required to be our best.
If schedules dictate rising early, get some rest.
Work not done will wait another day
And, we must not forget to balance work with play.

Children think adults can do no wrong,
If we teach them balance we teach them to be strong.
We model for our kids everyday.
They see what we do, how we behave, when we pray.

To reduce the struggles, fears and strife
Understand the important balance in one's life.
As we face challenge along the way,
We can teach it forward, how to live work and play.

MOUNTAIN WONDERLAND

Snow covered white silhouettes of peaks and trees.
Clean outlined houses, with lights on by degrees.
I drive around the mountain in the moonlight
As the pure white snow lights up the winter night.

While looking down on the quaint village below
Smoke billows up from chimney tops in a row.
Lights are shining through the snowflake-etched window
Of many houses beneath the fallen snow.

No cars out except for me this winter night.
Quiet, serene, peaceful, my senses delight.
This scene will remain in my memories eye
As a place to revisit as years go by.

Branches heavy laden with the fallen snow
Bend and sparkle in moonlight as they hang low.
Not a heavy snow that breaks trees and branches,
Light fluffy snow that reflects and enhances.

Lovely to look at, wonder and meditate
The problems of the world or of my own fate.
To see the world so calm on a mountain top,
A posh mental retreat for a future stop.

DESERTED CHILD

My first memory of love was for mom and dad.
When dad would come home, he had a quarter for me.
Bought mom's cup of coffee with that quarter I had.
Mom had her boarding house and dad went back to sea.

Dad, a tuna fisherman, was gone more and more.
He took brother and me to see his ship one day.
Mom and dad had separated when I was four.
Wanted to live with dad, but not for me to say.

Mom married four more times and we lost track of dad.
Dad would marry once more and then go back to sea.
Mom would have nine children and gave it all she had.
Dad had one more baby boy with wife number three.

Mom had an extremely hard time financially.
And we would even search for dad, for child support.
Sadly, dad's ship was captured and ransomed at sea.
The President gave him a plaque, once back at port.

Years later, when my handsome only son was born,
I had a break-up of my own with my son's dad.
Got a great job in communications one morn.
Selling long-distance and Internet wasn't bad.

On a search engine people-search I did explore.
Looking for dad saw my step-grandmother online.
Grandma told me my dad had died two years before
And told me about dad's son, a brother of mine.

Found our sibling in Oregon all a quiver.
He told me dad had died without reason or rhyme.
A grim disease called cirrhosis of the liver,
That many seamen die of before it's their time.

Dad told my half-brother to look us up and yet,
Although my only son spoke with his only son,
It has been thirteen years, and we have never met.
But, we e-mail and call each other just for fun.

Through pictures we would know each other's face by sight.
Some say you can see the family resemblance.
Maybe someone will someday take an airplane flight
To meet and to exchange a big hug and a glance.

Mom passed away last year when she was eighty-four
Still just as beautiful as in her pageant days.
She always lived her life on her own terms and more.
And she taught us how to live by learning her ways.

Mom's fight held a collapsed heart artery in store
However, it did not take her life on that day.
She probably thought she could fight death just once more.
But after five painful months, mother passed away.

She nurtured a strong family bond, at such a cost
Bravely struggling to keep us all together.
Not unscathed, sometimes she won and sometimes she lost.
She always came back and tried to make things better.

Deserted by parents, grandparents, spouse and friend,
And for some, cherished siblings have since passed away.
We love the past, live in the present, and defend,
Those revered living on in our hearts every day.

LIFE'S TIME LINE

As babies we are fragile and so dependant on those
Who haven't a clue or, who can be loving and composed.
If we the terrible two's and adolescence survive
We may learn what is happening and take over our lives.

Growing up we are competitive and learn how to test.
After all, our hopeful parents expect only the best.
We learn to work and play hard, and do not want to be last
And it is so important we win, and childhood goes fast.

As young adults we seek notice, and we love all our wins.
Wanting approval from others, needing time with our friends
To help us with self-esteem, and to not be so lonely,
As we dream of a true love to be our one and only.

And once in our new careers, we will compete for best jobs.
The competition gets fierce and we get lost in the cogs
Of the never ending life struggle to get to the top,
The proverbial lack of free time, and work that won't stop.

Then at mid-life, we support lifestyles and families we love.
Still thinking of late parents who are abiding above.
Can we make a difference in the lives of others we meet?
Wanting to retire in comfort, and give back to the weak.

Sadly, we approach our senior years with gray in our hair.
Retirement too far away and we think it's not fair
That our bodies are wearing out and it really seems sad
To have more aches, pains, and work with fewer funds to be had.

As seniors we fear age, immobility, and wrinkle.
Who dares to care for us now and, will we lose our twinkle?
Will our bodies eventually give out before our mind?
Or, will we forget all we know, and will people be kind?

In retrospect, life's time-line is quite a roller coaster
With ups and downs you might visualize on a wall-poster.
But, with God's help and guidance, and yes, the patience of Job
We survive life's timetable peaks, and the unforeseen low.

REJOICE

The storm is over.
A dark cloud still looms,
But sunshine's coming
To flourish the blooms.

The cold wind and rain
And chill's gone away,
To bestow us with
A most wondrous day.

So thrilling the warmth
To be felt by all,
Touting spring is here
Mother Nature's call.

To feel such stillness
And witness the dawn,
As daybreak alerts
Many birds in song.

Life begins again
Rejoice make new plans,
With a vibrant sky
All across the lands.

WALKING THE DOG

While walking Chance, my dog
A slow rabbit passed by
My walk became a jog
The dog's spirits were high.

My flip-flops start to slide
In the gravel indeed.
I go up like a ride,
Then let loose of the lead.

And down on my elbow
In the gravel I moan.
I collapse, didn't know,
Broke my humerus bone.

My arm is now broken
And my blood pressure's high,
As harsh words were spoken
Hurt, in shock as I cry.

Screamed and cried by the tree
As my dog came around,
Worried looking at me
Rabbit's not to be found.

It was not my dog's fault
A big puppy that's all,
The challenge of the chase
And angle of the fall.

I will still walk my dog
But if he picks up speed,
Chasing rabbit or frog,
I'll turn loose of the lead.

I can gather him up
Sometime after the chase.
And I don't blame the pup
As he's licking my face.

IT'S A BEAUTIFUL DAY

"It's a beautiful day outside!"
Whispers circulate round the room.
We continue to work with pride
But, the feelings are those of gloom.

We are working our ten-hour shift
Or some people only work eight.
AM traffic at dawn was swift
Rush all day, returning home late.

A lunch and two breaks are too short
To stroll in the ambiance, true.
So we muse and spread the report
Of sunshine and heavens so blue.

On our day off we're too tired
To entertain outside and then
The weekend is over too soon
And it starts all over again.

SMELLS IN THE WORKPLACE

The smell of popcorn at work can tickle your nose
Like somewhere, it is being burnt on some workdays.
It can make you take notice and stand on your toes
Looking for the 'big cart' through the cubical maze.

There are office desks and room dividers within
The guarded call center where I just started work.
And many workers and endless phone calls come in
Forming a way of life, with a sporadic quirk.

Each department of workers or agents in vain
Have celebrations, clap for each other with glee.
Omitting their co-workers not feeling their pain,
New employees wonder, "Why don't they include me?"

Different departments have twenty people or more
Working for companies and answering the phone.
Research, data entry, computers they explore,
People learning their jobs as their talents they hone.

A savory roast beef aroma fills the room.
Someone gets an early lunch, and we can now smell
Spicy, mouth-watering, smokehouse smells as they loom,
Along with the fragrant smell of burnt-side-of-cow.

Wonder how in the world that small smoked beef sandwich
Can make me as hungry as I have ever been?
I wonder if they saw me look, or felt my twitch.
Coveting the smell of a lunch...is that a sin?

Now smell the chicken, like in a rotisserie!
A fried chicken place across the road has a store.
People bring back their lunch, eating right next to me.
Late lunch has me hungry, looking round the room more.

What's more, some people eat well some don't eat at all.
We've no time for lunch, and sit next to each other.
And we're trying to work, as our thoughts hit the wall.
With smells such as these, concentration they smother.

Employee's lunches are staggered which is the key.
Eating spans for hours, and smells float among us.
It's the paycheck we're there for and, lunch isn't free.
And support for bring-a-dish-day is too much fuss.

The popcorn machine's again working and smelly
As the butter smell once more permeates the room.
"Only the best smell in the world!" says my belly.
It is crying for popcorn in this work-place tomb.

I'm told that the popcorn is for a different group,
Not for data-entry but for trainees it seems.
Eating popcorn is special. We're not in the loop.
So, we only get smells and buttered popcorn dreams.

It doesn't taste as good as it smells anyway.
Sometimes the salty popcorn gets stuck in our teeth,
In the fillings, or gums, irritating all day.
What matters if we don't get what's out of our reach?

I usually bring lunch, a sandwich I take in
After all, I must work and I save money too.
Something not too smelly, wait...do I smell BACON???
Company coffee's free, I can smell the fresh brew!

The End